Playin

Keeping Kids Entertained

INDOORS

Age group 4 to 12 years old

Simi Subhramanian

For permissions requests, write to the publisher at the address below:

Publisher: Simi Subhramanian, India

Email: shaurisimi@gmail.com

Cover design by Simi Subhramanian

Disclaimer: The activities and games provided in this book are intended to keep kids entertained indoors and are targeted for children aged 4 to 12 years old.

The safety and supervision of children during playtime are the responsibility of parents, guardians, or responsible adults. The author and publisher disclaim any liability for any injury, accident, or harm that may occur during the implementation of the activities and games.

The activities described in this book are meant to provide fun and engaging experiences for children while indoors. However, individual preferences, abilities, and developmental stages may vary. It is essential to adapt the activities to suit each child's age and capabilities.

The reader is encouraged to use the activities and games in this book responsibly and to ensure that they align with the child's interests and needs. Additionally, it is essential to create a safe environment for play and adhere to any safety guidelines recommended by manufacturers of toys or materials used in the activities.

Author Profile

Simi Subhramanian is an accomplished author and dedicated educator with a passion for teaching. She holds a range of qualifications in the teaching profession, including certifications from the Asian College of Teachers, TQUK (Training Qualifications UK), and Montessori Europe. With an extensive educational background, Simi brings a wealth of knowledge and expertise to her writing.

Simi's journey in education began at the Asian College of Teachers in Mumbai, India. There, she honed her teaching skills and gained a deep understanding of pedagogical principles. Armed with this foundation, she embarked on a mission to inspire and educate students of all ages through her writing.

Further enriching her qualifications, Simi pursued additional certifications from TQUK and Montessori Europe. These certifications expanded her repertoire of teaching methodologies and deepened her understanding of diverse learning styles. With these enhanced skills, she has been able to create engaging and effective educational content that caters to a wide range of learners.

Simi's writing reflects her commitment to excellence in education. She understands that effective teaching goes beyond imparting knowledge; it requires creativity, empathy, and the ability to connect with students on a deeper level. Her dedication to fostering a love of learning and promoting critical thinking is evident in her work.

Through her writing, Simi aims to inspire and empower students, encouraging them to reach their full potential. Her books and educational materials cover a wide range of subjects, from language arts to science and mathematics. Simi's approach emphasizes active learning, interactivity, and real-world applications to ensure students grasp concepts thoroughly.

With her diverse qualifications and years of experience in the teaching profession, Simi Subhramanian has established herself as a trusted and respected author in the education field. Her passion for teaching shines through in her writing, making her work both informative and engaging.

Simi continues to stay abreast of the latest developments in education and actively seeks innovative teaching approaches. By incorporating emerging trends and methodologies into her writing, she ensures that her educational materials remain relevant and effective.

Simi Subhramanian's author profile represents a seamless integration of her teaching qualifications from the Asian College of Teachers, TQUK, and Montessori Europe. Her expertise and dedication make her a valuable asset in the realm of educational literature, as she strives to make a positive impact on students' lives through her insightful and engaging content.

Introduction

Unlock the gateway to a world where laughter echoes through hallways, and imaginations soar to extraordinary heights. Welcome to "Playing Games: Keeping Kids Entertained Indoors," a captivating treasure trove of joyous adventures designed for children aged 4 to 12 years old. In this book, the walls of your home will transform into a vibrant canvas of possibilities, where playtime knows no bounds, and cherished memories are waiting to be made.

As parents, guardians, or educators, we are entrusted with the responsibility of nurturing the sparks of creativity and wonder within young minds. In today's digital age, where screens vie for their attention, fostering an environment of engaging indoor play becomes paramount to their growth and development. This book is your secret weapon, your wellspring of inspiration, and your guiding light to unlocking the full potential of indoor playtime.

For the eager 4 to 6-year-olds, embark on a magical journey of discovery as we present a delightful collection of imaginative and interactive games. Watch as they build their first forts, partake in whimsical scavenger hunts, and create masterpieces in an arts and crafts wonderland. Every page brims with enchanting activities carefully curated to ignite their curiosity and instil a love for learning through play.

As we venture deeper into the heart of this book, we find the curious minds of 7 to 9-year-olds eagerly awaiting the challenges that lie ahead. Witness their laughter and excitement as they engage in active games, leaping over imaginary obstacles in an obstacle course extravaganza or competing in friendly balloon volleyball matches. But the fun doesn't end there - educational games and mind-bending puzzles await to stimulate their intellect and expand their horizons.

For the older explorers, aged 10 to 12, our book presents an array of intriguing and technology-free games that foster camaraderie and togetherness. The thrill of classic card games, the infectious excitement of charades, and the strategic brilliance of DIY board games await, making every play-date an unforgettable bonding experience.

With raindrops tapping on the windows, fear not, for inside these pages, you'll discover a myriad of captivating activities to turn dreary days into cherished memories. Create indoor camping adventures, embark on movie marathons, or let their culinary prowess shine with delectable baking sessions - each day filled with delight and warmth.

We understand that with play comes challenges, and in these chapters, we offer insights on handling conflicts with compassion, nurturing sportsmanship, and finding a balance between technology and play. Embrace the ups and downs, for within the heart of these games, you'll uncover the essence of your child's unique personality and a deep bond that transcends the mere pages of this book.

So, gather around and immerse yourself in the enchanting world of "Playing Games: Keeping Kids Entertained Indoors." Let this book be your companion, your inspiration, and your guide on a journey of playtime wonder. With each turn of the page, watch as their eyes light up with anticipation, their laughter fills the room, and their hearts overflow with joy.

Together, let's build memories that will be etched in their hearts forever - memories of laughter, learning, and love. Let the adventure begin!

Chapter 1
Exploring the Magic of Indoor Play

A. Importance of Indoor Play for Kids

In a world bustling with digital distractions and fast-paced routines, the value of indoor play for children cannot be overstated. As the sun sets, and the stars emerge to sprinkle the night sky, our homes transform into sanctuaries of imagination and adventure. Indoor play, often overlooked amidst the allure of screens and gadgets, serves as a vital conduit for a child's holistic growth and development. Within the safe confines of our homes, indoor play nurtures the seeds of creativity, allowing young minds to bloom with unbridled expression. Through play, children are given the canvas to paint their dreams, weave fantastical tales, and create a world where anything is possible. As they immerse themselves in these magical realms, they develop critical thinking, problem-solving, and decision-making skills, laying the foundation for their future endeavours. Moreover, indoor play is a celebration of joy, an exuberant dance of laughter and delight that reverberates through the walls. It nourishes their emotional well-being, fostering resilience and self-confidence as they conquer challenges and celebrate triumphs. The bonds formed during playtime with family and friends become the cornerstone of lasting relationships, teaching them the essence of cooperation, empathy, and camaraderie.

B. Benefits of Playing Games Indoors

Playing games indoors, with its myriad of benefits, serves as a gateway to a world where education and entertainment intertwine seamlessly. As children engage in these purposeful activities, they unlock a trove of cognitive, physical, and emotional advantages that enrich their lives in profound ways.

Cognitive Stimulation: Indoor games challenge their minds, enhancing memory retention, concentration, and problem-solving skills. From exciting puzzles to thought-provoking trivia, each game presents an opportunity to learn, discover, and expand their intellectual horizons.

Physical Development: While the great outdoors may beckon for physical play, indoor games offer their unique advantages. Children partake in active games that enhance their motor skills, balance, and coordination, ensuring a healthy and active lifestyle.

Emotional Well-being: Laughter becomes a symphony, and smiles light up every room as children immerse themselves in the joys of indoor play. This emotional release fosters a sense of happiness, reducing stress and anxiety, and

instilling a positive outlook on life.

Educational Engagement: Through educational games and activities, children embrace learning as an exhilarating adventure. Whether discovering the wonders of science, diving into the realms of geography, or embarking on mathematical quests, knowledge becomes a thrilling pursuit.

Screen-time Moderation: Indoor play serves as a delightful alternative to excessive screen time, providing a healthier balance between technological engagements and real-world interactions.

C. Setting Up an Indoor Play Area

Creating a dedicated indoor play area is the cornerstone of transforming your home into a wonderland of exploration and fun. Designate a cozy corner or a spacious room where their imaginations can take flight without boundaries. Fill it with age-appropriate toys, art supplies, and educational resources that cater to their interests and developmental stages. Consider the safety aspect, ensuring the play area is free from potential hazards and sharp edges. Childproof the space while still allowing room for creativity and exploration.

As you embark on this enchanting journey of indoor play, remember that each moment spent together is a cherished gift. Let "Playing Games: Keeping Kids Entertained Indoors" be your companion in this delightful adventure, as you witness the magic unfold within the walls of your home. Embrace the joy, the wonder, and the boundless possibilities that indoor play brings forth, and let us embark on this captivating odyssey together.

Chapter 2
Active Games

A. Obstacle Course Challenge

Welcome to the heart-pounding realm of the "Obstacle Course Challenge," where young adventurers transform their homes into thrilling arenas of excitement and agility. This game unleashes a series of exhilarating obstacle courses that ignite their spirits, challenge their physical abilities, and spark their competitive fire.In a world where screens often dominate children's attention, the Obstacle Course Challenge offers a refreshing and invigorating alternative. With a little creativity and resourcefulness, household items become stepping stones, tunnels, and hurdles, transforming mundane spaces into daring courses of conquest. Children will tiptoe across cushions, crawl under tables, and hop between pillows as they navigate through the course. Each challenge they overcome strengthens their balance, flexibility, and coordination, fostering physical development in a fun and engaging way.

Setting up an obstacle course at home is a breeze, and it encourages children to explore their surroundings in innovative ways. As they create pathways through the living room, kitchen, and hallway, they become architects of their adventure, honing their spatial awareness and problem-solving skills. The Obstacle Course Challenge goes beyond physical prowess; it is an exercise in imaginative play and cognitive development. Children are not merely jumping over pillows or crawling under chairs; they are entering enchanted forests, crossing treacherous rivers, and embarking on epic quests. With every obstacle they conquer, their imaginations soar, creating elaborate narratives that unfold with each step they take. As they race against the clock or compete with friends and family, they experience the thrill of accomplishment and the joy of healthy competition. The Obstacle Course Challenge fosters a sense of determination and perseverance, teaching them the value of setting goals and striving to achieve them. Every successful leap and every triumph over a challenging obstacle reinforces their belief in their capabilities, empowering them to tackle challenges with confidence.

And the best part? The obstacle course can be redesigned and rearranged endlessly, offering an ever-changing canvas for their imagination to run wild. Children can challenge themselves with new obstacles or create themed courses

inspired by their favourite stories or movies. The possibilities are as boundless as their imagination, and each new iteration promises a fresh wave of excitement. Parents and caregivers can actively participate in this adventure, becoming fellow explorers in the whimsical world they've created. By engaging

in the Obstacle Course Challenge alongside their children, adults foster a sense of camaraderie and create cherished memories of shared playtime.

In a world that often places pressure on academic achievements and structured activities, the Obstacle Course Challenge serves as a reminder of the joy and importance of unstructured play. Through play, children learn valuable life skills, develop resilience, and form lasting bonds with their loved ones. As they laugh, cheer, and conquer each obstacle, they experience the pure essence of childhood joy.

B. Indoor Scavenger Hunt

Prepare for an adventure of mystery and discovery with the "Indoor Scavenger Hunt." In this game, children embark on a quest to unravel clues, solve riddles, and unearth hidden treasures within the cozy confines of their homes.

The Indoor Scavenger Hunt is not only an exercise in critical thinking but also a celebration of teamwork and camaraderie. As they collaborate with siblings or friends, children learn to communicate effectively, listen attentively, and appreciate the unique contributions of each team member. The beauty of the Indoor Scavenger Hunt lies in its versatility. Parents can tailor the hunt to suit the children's age, interests, and level of difficulty. For younger children, the clues can be simple and straightforward, leading them on a delightful adventure of discovery. As they grow older, the riddles can become more challenging, encouraging them to think creatively and strategically.

Crafting the scavenger hunt involves a touch of artistry, as parents strategically place clues throughout the house, leading children on a journey of exploration and surprise. Each clue solved brings them one step closer to the hidden treasure, and with each discovery, their eyes light up with wonder and joy. The excitement builds with each clue unravelled, and the atmosphere becomes charged with anticipation. The Indoor Scavenger Hunt is a game of suspense,

where children's enthusiasm and curiosity are in full bloom. As they follow the trail of hints, they enter a realm of imaginative play, envisioning themselves as intrepid explorers, detectives, or treasure hunters. This thrilling activity fosters a sense of achievement and accomplishment, boosting their self-esteem and instilling a belief in their abilities to overcome challenges. As they cheer for one another's discoveries, they learn the value of encouragement and support, creating a supportive and uplifting environment.

The Indoor Scavenger Hunt offers the perfect opportunity for educational

engagement. Through the clues and riddles, children can delve into a wide range of topics, from history and science to literature and math. Learning becomes a thrilling adventure, and they won't even realize they are absorbing knowledge along the way. Beyond the intellectual benefits, the Indoor Scavenger Hunt also cultivates essential social skills. Children learn to respect rules, follow fair play, and gracefully accept both victories and defeats. The sense of camaraderie formed during the hunt extends beyond the game itself, nurturing lasting friendships and bonds.

Indoor Scavenger Hunt can be adapted for various occasions and celebrations. Whether it's a rainy day or a special event like a birthday party, the hunt adds a touch of excitement and wonder to any gathering.

With the whole family or a group of friends on board, the Indoor Scavenger Hunt becomes a shared experience that strengthens connections and creates unforgettable memories.

C. Musical Chairs with a Twist

In this twist on a classic game, get ready to inject a burst of imagination and laughter into your playtime with "Musical Chairs with a Twist." Gather the little ones in a circle, and let the music guide them on a journey of playful fun. The whimsical nature of "Musical Chairs with a Twist" makes it an entertaining and engaging activity for children of all ages. It encourages creativity and spontaneity, as children eagerly embrace each task with enthusiasm. This game fosters a sense of playfulness and encourages children to let go of inhibitions, immersing themselves in the sheer joy of the moment. Moreover, "Musical Chairs with a Twist" is an excellent platform for imaginative play. The tasks can be tailored to suit any theme, from exploring outer space to embarking on an underwater adventure. This flexibility allows parents and caregivers to customize the game based on the children's interests, making it an ever-evolving experience that never loses its charm.

The game's inclusive nature ensures that every child remains an active participant throughout, eliminating any feelings of exclusion or disappointment. As children cheer for one another's performances, they learn the importance of encouragement and support, nurturing a positive and cooperative atmosphere.

Beyond the laughter and joy, "Musical Chairs with a Twist" instils valuable life skills in children. They learn to take turns, follow instructions, and exhibit good sportsmanship. The game becomes a platform for practising manners, patience, and grace, lessons that extend far beyond the playroom.

Parents and caregivers also play an essential role in fostering the joy of "Musical Chairs with a Twist." By enthusiastically participating and demonstrating their own sense of fun, adults set an example for children to follow. This shared experience creates moments of connection and strengthens the bond between children and caregivers.

D. Balloon Volleyball

Prepare for an action-packed adventure of "Balloon Volleyball," where children experience the thrill of a volleyball match without leaving the comfort of their home. Grab a few balloons, clear some space, and get ready for an epic showdown. The Balloon Volleyball is a dynamic and lively game that promotes physical activity and friendly competition. It enhances hand-eye coordination, agility, and reflexes as children leap and dive to keep the balloon in play. Additionally, it encourages teamwork and communication as players strategise and coordinate their movements to ensure a successful volley. Beyond the physical benefits, Balloon Volleyball cultivates essential social skills. Children learn to respect rules, follow fair play, and gracefully accept both victories and defeats. The sense of camaraderie formed during the game extends beyond the match itself, nurturing lasting friendships and bonds.

Balloon Volleyball's adaptability makes it an accessible and enjoyable game for children of all ages. Younger children can participate by using smaller balloons and engaging in less competitive play, while older children can engage in more intense rallies and strategise to outmanoeuvre their opponents. Parents and caregivers can actively participate in the game, serving as both referees and cheerleaders. By encouraging fair play and providing positive reinforcement, adults create an atmosphere of fun and encouragement, making Balloon Volleyball an experience filled with joy and camaraderie.

E. Indoor Bowling

Roll, aim, and strike! "Indoor Bowling" brings the excitement of the bowling alley right into your home. This game sets the stage for a striking adventure as children set up their own miniature bowling lanes using readily available items.

The joy of knocking down the pins in one swift roll fills the room with excitement and laughter. Children eagerly celebrate each strike and spare, and even the occasional miss becomes a chance for hilarious goofiness. Indoor Bowling creates a light-hearted and relaxed atmosphere, allowing everyone to enjoy the game without the pressure of competition.

While Indoor Bowling is undoubtedly loads of fun, it also offers numerous developmental benefits. Children enhance their hand-eye coordination, fine motor skills, and spatial awareness as they take aim and roll the "bowling ball." Each roll becomes an opportunity to learn and refine their technique, fostering a growth mindset and a willingness to try again. The game also presents opportunities for learning basic math skills. Children can tally scores, calculate points, and engage in simple addition as they keep track of their progress. This subtle integration of learning into play ensures that children absorb knowledge in a fun and effortless manner. Indoor Bowling's adaptability makes it suitable for children of different ages and skill levels. Younger children may enjoy simply rolling the ball and knocking down the pins, while older children can strategise to achieve a spare or even a strike.

Parents and caregivers can actively participate in Indoor Bowling, serving as both coaches and cheerleaders. By offering guidance on rolling techniques and celebrating each achievement, adults encourage a sense of accomplishment and boost children's self-confidence. Indoor Bowling is not just a game; it is an opportunity for quality family time and bonding. As families gather around the makeshift bowling alley, laughter fills the air, and memories are created that will be cherished for years to come.

In conclusion, the Active Games presented in this chapter offer a delightful array of playtime adventures that engage children's bodies, minds, and imaginations. From conquering challenging obstacle courses to unravelling clues in scavenger hunts, from dancing and performing in Musical Chairs to engaging in lively Balloon Volleyball matches, and from rolling strikes in Indoor Bowling to fostering cooperation and camaraderie among players, each game delivers unique experiences and valuable life lessons. These Active Games promote physical activity, cognitive development, and social interaction, encouraging a balanced and holistic approach to play. They offer an opportunity for parents, caregivers, and children to come together and create precious memories that build strong bonds and lasting connections.

In a world where technology often takes center stage, these games remind us of the joy and benefits of unstructured play. Through Active Games, children learn that play is not just about winning or achieving goals; it is about the process, the exploration, and the joy of simply being present in the moment. So, whether it's a rainy day, a holiday gathering, or a regular playtime with friends, let the Active Games reignite the spirit of playfulness and wonder in your home. Embrace the laughter, the cheers, and the joy that echo through the walls as

children dive into these delightful adventures. Together, let's create a world where indoor play becomes an unforgettable journey of exploration, growth, and limitless imagination.

Chapter 3

Creative Games

A. DIY Board Games

Welcome to the enchanting world of "DIY Board Games," where imagination and creativity merge to create unique and captivating play experiences. In this game , children embark on a thrilling journey of game design, crafting their own board games from scratch. DIY Board Games empower children to become game designers, artists, and storytellers all at once. Armed with a blank canvas and an abundance of art supplies, they can unleash their creativity to design game boards, create game pieces, and craft rules that reflect their wildest ideas and imaginations. The process begins with brainstorming, where children conceptualize the theme and mechanics of their games. They can draw inspiration from their favourite stories, adventures, or even their dreams. Whether it's an epic quest to save a magical kingdom, a treasure hunt through enchanted lands, or a space voyage to distant galaxies, the possibilities are as boundless as their imaginations.

Once the game concept is in place, children proceed to create the game board. They can use large sheets of cardboard or draw on poster paper to design their playing surface. With vibrant colours, markers, and stickers, they bring their imaginative worlds to life. Next comes the crafting of game pieces. Children can use clay, cardboard cut-outs, or even repurpose small toys to represent characters, objects, or tokens in their games. Each game piece becomes a unique expression of their artistic talents and personal flair. Finally, children craft the rules that govern their DIY board games. They decide how players move, what actions they can take, and how to win the game. As they fine-tune the rules, they develop critical thinking and problem-solving skills, learning how to create a balanced and enjoyable game experience for all players.

The joy of playing DIY Board Games extends beyond the creative process; it continues during gameplay. Children take pride in sharing their creations with friends and family, inviting them into their imaginative worlds. They experience the satisfaction of seeing their loved ones engaged and entertained by the games they have meticulously designed. DIY Board Games foster collaboration and cooperation, as players collectively navigate through the challenges and surprises laid out by the game's creator. With each roll of the dice or move of a game piece, the board game becomes a vessel for storytelling and shared adventures. Moreover, DIY Board Games are a beautiful way to celebrate individuality and foster self-expression. Each game reflects the unique personality and interests of its creator, making every play-through a celebration of their creativity and ingenuity.

As children experience the joy of game design, they may discover a newfound passion for art, storytelling, or game development. DIY Board Games open doors to various interests and possibilities, nurturing talents that may shape their future endeavours.

B. Arts and Crafts Corner

Enter the realm of "Arts and Crafts Corner," where a treasure trove of colourful materials awaits, and creativity knows no bounds. In this game, children unleash their artistic prowess, transforming simple materials into masterpieces that reflect their boundless imagination. The Arts and Crafts Corner is a sanctuary of self-expression, where children can explore various art forms and experiment with different techniques. With an assortment of art supplies such as paints, markers, coloured papers, glue, and beads, they have the freedom to create anything their hearts desire. One of the most captivating aspects of Arts and Crafts Corner is its versatility. Children can engage in a wide range of activities, from painting and drawing to collage-making and sculpting. They can immerse themselves in activities like making friendship bracelets, creating greeting cards, designing masks, or constructing paper mache sculptures.

Not only does Arts and Crafts Corner nurture artistic skills, but it also promotes fine motor skills and hand-eye coordination. As children cut, glue, and paint, they refine their dexterity and precision, enhancing their ability to control tools and materials. Art is a language of emotions, and the Arts and Crafts Corner allows children to express their feelings and experiences in a non-verbal manner. Whether they create cheerful, vibrant paintings or intricate, thoughtful collages, their artwork becomes a window into their inner worlds. Parents and caregivers play a significant role in fostering the joy of arts and crafts. By providing a supportive and encouraging environment, adults inspire children to explore their creativity and embrace artistic expression. Celebrating their creations and displaying their artwork in the home reinforces their sense of accomplishment and pride in their work.

The Arts and Crafts Corner is not just about the final product; it is also about the process. Children learn to embrace imperfections and view mistakes as opportunities for learning and growth. Each project becomes a journey of discovery, as they experiment with different techniques and learn from their experiences. Arts and Crafts Corner can also become a family activity, where parents and children come together to create art side by side.

Such shared experiences create bonds and build memories that children will cherish throughout their lives.

C. Puppet Show Extravaganza

Step into the magical world of "Puppet Show Extravaganza," where children bring their stories to life through the enchanting art of puppetry. In this game, a simple sock or a handcrafted puppet becomes a conduit for imaginative narratives and delightful performances. Puppetry has captivated audiences for centuries, and for children, it offers a unique opportunity to become storytellers, directors, and performers. Whether they create finger puppets, hand puppets, or marionettes, children can design their characters and imbue them with distinct personalities and voices. The Puppet Show Extravaganza begins with the creation of puppets. Children can craft characters from socks, paper bags, or even old socks and felt. With googly eyes, fabric scraps, and markers, they add personality to their puppets, transforming them into whimsical creatures or familiar animals.

Next, children design the stage for their puppet show. They can use a simple cardboard box, a curtain hung from a doorway, or even a specially crafted puppet theatre. Decorating the stage with colourful backdrops and props enhances the visual appeal and immerses the audience in the puppetry world.

As the puppeteers prepare for the show, they develop the storyline and script. Whether it's a fairy tale, a superhero adventure, or an original tale from their imagination, the story becomes the heart of the Puppet Show Extravaganza. Children can collaborate with friends or family members to weave a captivating narrative that unfolds on the puppet theatre. During the performance, children step into the roles of their puppets' voices, controlling their movements and interacting with other puppet characters. The art of puppetry encourages public speaking and self-confidence as children present their stories to an eager audience.

The Puppet Show Extravaganza is not just a form of entertainment; it is a celebration of creativity and storytelling. It fosters children's ability to express themselves through storytelling, using puppets as vessels to communicate their ideas and emotions. This imaginative play nurtures empathy as children step into the shoes of their puppet characters and explore different perspectives. As they make decisions for their puppet characters and navigate the storyline, they learn to understand the motivations and feelings of others. Parents and caregivers play a supportive role in the Puppet Show Extravaganza, providing

encouragement and applause for the young puppeteers. By attending and engaging in the puppet shows, adults show that they value their children's creativity and efforts, inspiring them to continue exploring the enchanting world of puppetry. The Puppet Show Extravaganza also presents an opportunity for interdisciplinary learning. Children can incorporate elements of visual art, writing, and performance as they design their puppets, script the story, and act out the scenes. This multidisciplinary approach enriches their understanding of various forms of expression.

D. Storytelling Time

Gather around for "Storytelling Time," a game that celebrates the timeless tradition of oral storytelling. In a world of digital entertainment, storytelling holds a special place, transporting children to far-off lands and sparking their imaginations. Storytelling is an art that has been passed down through generations, and this game encourages children to become storytellers themselves. With each tale they spin, they hone their storytelling skills, captivating their audience with vivid descriptions and engaging narratives.

The beauty of storytelling lies in its simplicity; all it requires is a captivated audience and a storyteller with a tale to tell. Children can share classic fairy tales, myths, or legends, or they can create original stories inspired by their own experiences and dreams.

As children dive into the world of storytelling, they develop their language and communication skills. They learn to use descriptive language to paint pictures in the minds of their listeners, engaging their senses and emotions. Storytelling fosters active listening in the audience, as children become enthralled by the unfolding tale. This attentive listening promotes concentration and focus, enhancing their ability to engage with narratives in various forms, such as books or audiobooks. Parents and caregivers can actively participate in Storytelling Time, either as storytellers or as avid listeners. By sharing stories from their own childhood or encouraging children to tell their tales, adults create an atmosphere of storytelling as a cherished family tradition. Storytelling Time is also an opportunity for children to explore different cultural traditions and stories from around the world. By sharing tales from various cultures, they learn to appreciate diversity and develop an understanding of different perspectives.

Furthermore, Storytelling Time can be combined with other creative activities, such as puppetry or arts and crafts. Children can create puppets to represent

characters from their stories or illustrate scenes from their narratives, enhancing their storytelling experience.

E. Build Your Own Fort

Prepare to embark on an adventure of "Building Your Own Fort," where children's creativity and resourcefulness are the guiding stars. In this game, household objects become the building blocks for constructing delightful hideaways and secret spaces. Building forts is a time-honoured childhood tradition, one that fosters imagination and provides a sense of ownership over one's space. Armed with blankets, pillows, cushions, and chairs, children can create their personal realms of magic and wonder. The fort-building process begins with a blank canvas, an open space where children can let their imaginations run wild. Using chairs and tables as the fort's foundation, they drape blankets and sheets over the furniture, transforming the structure into a cozy hideaway.

Once the fort is erected, it becomes a blank canvas for customization. Children can decorate the interior with pillows, stuffed animals, fairy lights, and drawings, creating an ambiance that reflects their unique personalities and tastes. Building forts encourages teamwork and collaboration among siblings or friends. As they work together to construct their fortress, they learn to communicate, compromise, and appreciate each other's ideas and contributions.

The fort becomes a haven for creative play, where children's imagination takes center stage. It becomes a castle, a spaceship, a pirate ship, or a cozy reading nook. With each new day, the fort can transform into a different world, adapting to the ever-changing whims of its young occupants. Beyond the joy of building, forts become a place for storytelling, role-playing, and imaginative adventures. Children can create narratives and scenarios that unfold within the fort's walls, exploring imaginary landscapes and enacting fantastical quests.

Parents and caregivers play a supportive role in fort-building, offering guidance and assistance as needed. By joining in the construction process or engaging in imaginative play within the fort, adults demonstrate the value they place on their children's creative endeavours. Building forts is not only a fun activity but also a form of constructive play that nurtures problem-solving skills. As children design and assemble the structure, they learn about stability, balance, and spatial relationships, applying principles of engineering and architecture in a playful context. The fort becomes a refuge where children can retreat, unwind, and let their imaginations soar. It provides a sense of ownership and

independence, as they create and curate their special space. In a world where technology often dominates leisure time, fort-building offers a refreshing and simple escape into the realm of imagination. It celebrates the beauty of unstructured play and encourages children to create their own magical worlds, reminding us all that the most extraordinary adventures often happen within the walls of a home-made fort.

In conclusion, the Creative Games presented in this chapter unlock the boundless potential of children's creativity, sparking their imaginations, and celebrating the joy of self-expression.

Chapter 4
Educational Games

In the realm of "Educational Games," playtime and learning converge in a delightful dance of exploration and discovery. This chapter offers a treasure trove of games that not only entertain but also stimulate young minds, fostering a love for learning and intellectual growth.

A. Math and Word Puzzles

Prepare to embark on a thrilling journey of numbers and words with the "Math and Word Puzzles" adventure. In this game, children unravel the mysteries of math and language through engaging puzzles that challenge their problem-solving skills and critical thinking. Math puzzles come in various forms, from classic Sudoku to number crosswords and logic puzzles. These brain-teasing activities encourage children to think logically, analyse patterns, and apply mathematical concepts to arrive at solutions. As they solve puzzles, they develop a deeper understanding of arithmetic, spatial reasoning, and deductive reasoning. Word puzzles, on the other hand, immerse children in the fascinating world of language and vocabulary. Crossword puzzles, word searches, and anagrams are just a few examples of the word-based fun that awaits. These activities enrich children's language skills, improve their spelling, and enhance their ability to recognize and manipulate words.

The beauty of math and word puzzles lies in their adaptability to different age groups and skill levels. Parents and caregivers can tailor the difficulty level of the puzzles to suit the children's abilities, ensuring that each challenge is engaging yet achievable. This personalized approach encourages a sense of accomplishment and boosts self-confidence as children successfully solve each puzzle. Furthermore, math and word puzzles can become a delightful family activity. Parents and children can work together to solve puzzles, fostering collaboration and communication as they exchange ideas and strategies. This joint effort creates moments of connection and shared achievement. Beyond the pure enjoyment of puzzle-solving, these educational games offer tangible cognitive benefits. They enhance children's memory, concentration, and attention to detail, skills that are valuable in both academic and daily life settings. The problem-solving mindset cultivated through math and word puzzles extends to other areas of learning, nurturing a lifelong love for inquiry and discovery.

B. Science Experiments at Home

Welcome to the captivating world of "Science Experiments at Home," where

children become curious scientists, conducting hands-on experiments and unravelling the wonders of the natural world. In this game, the home becomes a laboratory of exploration, where everyday items transform into scientific tools of discovery. Science experiments offer a unique blend of fun and education, as children engage their senses, curiosity, and creativity. With simple materials like baking soda, vinegar, water, and food colouring, they can create fascinating reactions and learn about chemical changes. One classic experiment is the volcanic eruption, where children mix baking soda and vinegar to produce a bubbly and fizzy reaction. This activity not only captivates their attention but also teaches them about the basics of chemical reactions and gas release.

Water-based experiments, such as floating and sinking, introduce children to the concept of buoyancy and density. By experimenting with different objects and liquids, they observe how some materials float effortlessly while others sink. Science experiments at home also extend to the realm of physics, where children explore the principles of motion and force. Activities like making paper air-planes or building simple catapults introduce concepts like aerodynamics and projectile motion in a playful and tangible manner. The process of conducting experiments fosters the scientific method, as children form hypotheses, make observations, and draw conclusions from their findings. This approach nurtures critical thinking and cultivates a spirit of inquiry, encouraging children to question and seek answers to the mysteries of the natural world.

Parents and caregivers play an essential role in supporting science experiments at home. By encouraging children's curiosity and offering guidance during the process, adults create an environment where scientific exploration is celebrated and valued. Science experiments offer a bridge between theoretical knowledge and practical application. Children can relate scientific principles to real-life phenomena, making learning relevant and relatable. This hands-on approach also piques their interest in science as they witness the magic of cause and effect.

C. Geography Trivia

Prepare to embark on a thrilling journey around the world with "Geography Trivia," an adventure that tests children's knowledge of continents, countries, and cultures. In this game, children become globetrotters, exploring the diverse landscapes and rich histories of our planet.

Geography trivia games present an opportunity to broaden children's horizons and develop their understanding of the world's diverse regions. By asking questions about capitals, landmarks, flags, and geographical features, the games offer a captivating way to learn about different countries and their unique attributes. The trivia questions can cover a range of topics, from historical events and famous landmarks to traditional cuisines and cultural practices. As children answer questions and learn new facts, they develop a deeper appreciation for the rich tapestry of cultures that make up our global community. Geography trivia games can be played in various formats, from traditional question-and-answer sessions to interactive quizzes with maps and visual aids. These games not only reinforce geographical knowledge but also enhance children's memory and retention skills.

As children delve into the fascinating world of geography, they become global citizens with a broader perspective on the interconnectedness of our world. They develop empathy and understanding for different cultures and recognize the importance of preserving our planet's natural beauty and resources. Parents and caregivers can actively participate in Geography Trivia games, offering support and sharing their own knowledge about different countries and cultures. By celebrating the diversity of our world, adults create an atmosphere of inclusivity and promote global awareness. Moreover, Geography Trivia games can be adapted to suit different age groups and levels of knowledge. From simple questions about countries and capitals to more advanced queries about historical events and demographics, children can engage with the games at a level that is both enjoyable and challenging.

D. Memory and Matching Games

Welcome to the realm of "Memory and Matching Games," where children engage their minds and sharpen their memory skills through playful challenges. In this game, the home becomes a stage for memory mastery as children match pairs of cards, tiles, or objects in an exciting race against time. Memory games are not only enjoyable but also offer valuable cognitive benefits. As children search for matching pairs, they exercise their short-term memory, attention to detail, and visual-spatial skills. These skills are crucial for academic success, as they support learning in subjects like mathematics, reading comprehension, and problem-solving.

Memory games come in various forms, from classic card-matching to tile-based games like Mahjong. Whether it's flipping over cards to find matching pictures

or aligning tiles with identical patterns, the games captivate children's attention and encourage them to stay focused. The adaptability of memory games makes them suitable for children of different ages and developmental stages. Younger children can start with simpler games with fewer cards, while older children can tackle more complex challenges with larger sets. Parents and caregivers can actively participate in memory games, either as playmates or as cheerleaders. By engaging in the games together, adults create moments of bonding and shared enjoyment, reinforcing the idea that learning is a joyful and collaborative experience. Memory games also provide a break from screens and technology, offering a screen-free alternative for leisure and entertainment. In a world where digital devices are ubiquitous, these analog games remind us of the joy of tactile play and the benefits of focusing on the present moment.

E. Indoor Alphabet Hunt

Prepare for an exciting treasure hunt of letters and words with the "Indoor Alphabet Hunt," an adventure that introduces young learners to the wonders of the alphabet. In this game, children become explorers, searching for hidden letters and discovering words that lurk in the nooks and crannies of their home.

The Indoor Alphabet Hunt is a delightful way to introduce the alphabet to preschoolers and early learners. Children embark on a quest to find and identify letters in their environment, whether on objects, books, or everyday items. This hands-on approach brings the alphabet to life, making learning engaging and interactive. The hunt can be adapted to different levels of knowledge, making it suitable for children at various stages of their alphabet journey. Younger learners can focus on identifying letters, while older children can search for specific words that begin with each letter. The alphabet hunt encourages children to be attentive and observant, as they scan their surroundings for hidden letters. This sharpens their visual discrimination skills, helping them differentiate between similar-looking letters and refine their letter recognition.

Parents and caregivers play a crucial role in the Indoor Alphabet Hunt, guiding children in their search and offering praise for their discoveries. By creating a positive and encouraging environment, adults instil a sense of accomplishment and foster a love for learning. Moreover, the alphabet hunt can be combined with storytelling, as children create narratives based on the objects or words they find. This imaginative play nurtures language development and storytelling abilities, encouraging children to express themselves creatively. The Indoor Alphabet Hunt is not limited to a single play session; it can become an ongoing

adventure as children continue to discover new letters and words in different corners of their home. This sense of continuity and discovery transforms learning into an exciting and continuous journey.

In conclusion, the Educational Games presented in this chapter blend play and learning, offering children a delightful journey of discovery and intellectual growth. From solving math and word puzzles to conducting science experiments at home, from exploring geography trivia to engaging in memory and matching games, and from embarking on an Indoor Alphabet Hunt to unravelling the wonders of language, each game presents a unique opportunity to cultivate curiosity, critical thinking, and a love for learning. As children immerse themselves in these educational adventures, they develop essential life skills, from problem-solving and critical thinking to communication and collaboration. Moreover, these games go beyond the confines of formal education; they cultivate a mindset of lifelong learning, encouraging children to remain curious and inquisitive about the world around them.

So, let the magic of Educational Games infuse playtime with the joy of discovery and the wonder of learning. As children engage their minds and hearts in these captivating activities, they set forth on a path of intellectual exploration that will shape their journey of growth and discovery for years to come.

Chapter 5
Technology-Free Games

In the enchanting world of "Technology-Free Games," children step away from screens and electronic devices to embark on a delightful journey of play, imagination, and human connection. This chapter offers a plethora of timeless and engaging games that celebrate the joy of unstructured play and bring people together in moments of laughter and camaraderie.

A. Classic Card Games

Prepare to shuffle, deal, and strategise as we delve into the realm of "Classic Card Games," where a simple deck of cards transforms into a gateway of fun and excitement. In this game, children of all ages can enjoy a variety of card games that hone their cognitive skills, promote fair play, and foster friendly competition. The classic deck of cards holds a treasure trove of game options, from well-known games like Go Fish and Crazy Eights to more complex games like Poker and Bridge. Each game introduces children to different card values, suits, and game mechanics, offering a diverse and engaging experience. Card games are not only a source of amusement but also a valuable educational tool. As children play, they practice important math skills, such as counting, addition, and probability. They develop strategic thinking as they plan their moves and anticipate the actions of other players.

Furthermore, card games promote social interaction and communication. Players engage in lively discussions, make negotiations, and experience the camaraderie of shared experiences. These interactions foster sportsmanship and teach children to both win and lose gracefully. Card games can be adapted to suit different age groups and skill levels, making them an accessible and enjoyable activity for the entire family. Younger children can learn simple games with fewer rules, while older children can delve into more complex games that require strategic thinking and planning. Parents and caregivers play an essential role in the world of Classic Card Games, serving as teachers and playmates. By guiding children in the rules and strategies of each game, adults create an environment of learning and collaboration. Moreover, card games offer a welcome respite from the digital world, providing an opportunity for face-to-face interaction and meaningful connections. As children gather around a table, the atmosphere becomes one of laughter, concentration, and shared enjoyment.

B. Charades and Pictionary

Welcome to the realm of "Charades and Pictionary," where words transform

into gestures and drawings become the language of play. In this game, children immerse themselves in the world of pantomime and sketching, unleashing their creativity and imagination in a game of wordplay and guessing.

Charades is a classic party game where players act out words or phrases without speaking while their teammates guess the answers. This game not only encourages creativity and non-verbal communication but also builds empathy as players try to understand each other's gestures. The joy of Charades lies in the spontaneity of the performance and the hilarity that ensues when gestures are misinterpreted or interpreted in unexpected ways. Players find themselves laughing together as they navigate through the whimsical and sometimes unpredictable world of pantomime. Pictionary, on the other hand, invites players to express words or phrases through drawings. Armed with a drawing board and markers, children bring their artistic skills to the forefront, translating abstract concepts into visual representations.

Pictionary enhances visual-spatial skills and creativity, as players must think quickly and creatively to depict words in a limited amount of time. It fosters teamwork as players collaborate to decipher drawings and guess the correct answers. Both Charades and Pictionary promote active participation, as players take turns performing and guessing, creating an atmosphere of excitement and anticipation. These games transcend language barriers and create a shared language of gestures and sketches that bring people together in joyful play.

Parents and caregivers can actively participate in Charades and Pictionary, joining in the fun as teammates or enthusiastic observers. By celebrating each performance and offering encouragement, adults foster an atmosphere of playfulness and camaraderie.

C. Simon Says

Get ready to listen, follow, and giggle with "Simon Says," a game that challenges children's listening skills and ability to follow instructions. In this game, children become attentive players, waiting for the command of "Simon Says" before carrying out actions. Simon Says is a classic game of obedience and attention, where one player takes on the role of "Simon" and gives instructions to the other players. The twist is that players should only follow the instructions if they begin with the phrase "Simon Says." The game becomes a delightful challenge as players navigate between following and resisting instructions. The excitement builds as "Simon" tries to trick the other players with clever commands, causing bursts of laughter when participants make mistakes.

Simon Says enhances listening and concentration skills, as players must pay close attention to each command to determine whether they should act upon it. This ability to focus on verbal cues is a valuable skill that extends beyond the game into various aspects of daily life. The game fosters social interaction and leadership, as players take turns being "Simon" and guiding the group. As the leader, children practice clear communication and gain confidence in directing others. Simon Says can be played indoors or outdoors, making it a versatile and accessible game for any setting. Its simplicity and ease of play make it an excellent choice for spontaneous play or planned group activities. Parents and caregivers can participate in Simon Says, taking turns being "Simon" or joining in the fun as players. By engaging in the game, adults create a sense of playfulness and shared enjoyment, strengthening the bond between family members or friends.

D. Hide and Seek with a Twist

Prepare for an adventure of "Hide and Seek with a Twist," where the classic game of hiding and seeking takes on new dimensions and imaginative variations. In this game, children become masterful hiders and seekers as they explore creative ways to play the timeless game. Hide and Seek is a beloved game that has entertained generations of children. However, to add a twist to the traditional version, children can introduce variations that enhance the fun and excitement. One variant is "Sardines," where one player hides while the others seek. However, when a seeker finds the hider, instead of announcing the discovery, they quietly join them in their hiding spot. The game continues until all the seekers have found the hiding spot, culminating in a joyful and crowded hiding place.

Another twist is "Flash-light Hide and Seek," where the seeker uses a flash-light to find the hiders in a darkened room or outdoor area. The thrill of being spotted by the beam of light adds an extra layer of excitement to the game. Hide and Seek can be played indoors or outdoors, offering children the flexibility to choose their favourite setting. Whether they hide behind furniture, under beds, or among trees in the backyard, the game becomes a thrilling escapade of discovery and surprise. This game of hide and seek fosters physical activity and exploration, as children search for the perfect hiding spots and navigate through different environments. It encourages children to appreciate the wonders of their surroundings, whether it's the nooks and crannies of their home or the beauty of nature in the outdoors. Parents and caregivers can join in the fun of Hide and Seek with a Twist, either as participants or as enthusiastic observers.

By celebrating the clever hiding spots and cheering on the seekers, adults create an atmosphere of playfulness and shared enjoyment.

E. Indoor Picnic Party

Step into a world of "Indoor Picnic Party," where the magic of picnics comes alive within the comfort of your home. In this g, children create a charming picnic setting indoors, complete with delicious treats, fun activities, and quality time with loved ones. The Indoor Picnic Party offers a delightful alternative to traditional dining, as children lay out blankets or cushions to create a cozy picnic spot in the living room or any indoor space. They can invite family members, friends, or even their favourite toys to join in the picnic festivities. Picnic baskets and lunch-boxes become the vessels of delectable delights, as children fill them with finger foods, sandwiches, fruits, and refreshing drinks. The picnic menu can be as elaborate or as simple as desired, allowing children to express their culinary creativity.

During the picnic, children can engage in a variety of fun activities, such as storytelling, playing board games, or simply enjoying each other's company. The picnic setting creates an ambiance of relaxation and togetherness, fostering memorable moments of connection and laughter. The Indoor Picnic Party is an opportunity for children to play host and hostess, as they take on roles of welcoming their guests and serving the picnic treats. This experience nurtures social skills and empathy, as children learn to care for the needs and preferences of others. Parents and caregivers play an essential role in the Indoor Picnic Party, participating as guests and enjoying the imaginative play created by their children. By valuing the effort and creativity put into organizing the picnic, adults create an atmosphere of celebration and joy. Furthermore, the Indoor Picnic Party is an opportunity to celebrate the small joys of life and appreciate the simple pleasures of shared moments with loved ones. It reinforces the idea that meaningful connections can be fostered through simple, technology-free activities that encourage face-to-face interactions.

In conclusion, the world of Technology-Free Games offers an enchanting array of play experiences that celebrate the joy of unstructured play and human connection. From the strategic card games to the creative world of Charades and Pictionary, from the attentive listening of Simon Says to the imaginative twists of Hide and Seek, and from the indoor picnics that bring people together in celebration, each game invites children to explore the magic of play without the need for screens or devices.

As children engage in these timeless games, they develop essential life skills, from critical thinking and communication to teamwork and empathy. Moreover, the world of Technology-Free Games reminds us all of the beauty of unplugged play, fostering a sense of presence and connection in a world that is often dominated by technology. So, let the charm of Technology-Free Games infuse playtime with laughter, imagination, and shared experiences. As children immerse themselves in these delightful activities, they rediscover the joy of human connection and the wonders of play beyond the confines of screens and gadgets.

Chapter 6
Rainy Day Activities

Rainy days need not be gloomy affairs, they present the perfect opportunity for "Rainy Day Activities," where children can embark on exciting indoor adventures filled with creativity, entertainment, and joy. In this chapter, we explore a collection of delightful activities that brighten up even the dreariest of days, making rainy days a reason to celebrate rather than hide away.

A. Indoor Camping Adventure

Prepare for an "Indoor Camping Adventure," where children can experience the magic of camping without stepping foot outside their home. In this game, the living room transforms into a cozy campsite, complete with tents, sleeping bags, and all the trappings of a traditional camping trip. Creating an indoor campsite is a fun and interactive process. Children can set up makeshift tents using blankets and pillows, arranging them to create a cozy nook for their camping expedition. String lights or battery-operated lanterns add a touch of warmth and ambiance to the campsite. To complete the camping experience, children can gather around a pretend campfire made of paper or cardboard, where they can share stories and songs. Alternatively, a virtual campfire video on a screen can add a touch of realism to the indoor camping adventure.

During the indoor camping adventure, children can engage in various camping-themed activities. They can read camping-themed books or tell spooky stories by flash light, mimicking the age-old tradition of campfire tales. Indoor camping also provides an opportunity for stargazing, as children can create their own constellation charts and learn about the stars and planets. The wonders of the night sky come to life within the comfort of their indoor campsite. Parents and caregivers play an essential role in the Indoor Camping Adventure, supporting the imaginative play and creating a sense of excitement. By encouraging storytelling and participating in campfire activities, adults add to the magic of the camping experience. Moreover, the Indoor Camping Adventure fosters a spirit of adventure and exploration, encouraging children to embrace their imagination and creativity. It provides a safe and cozy space for imaginative play, reminding children that the wonders of nature and the joys of camping are always accessible, rain or shine.

B. Movie Marathon Day

Step into the world of "Movie Marathon Day," where children can immerse themselves in the magic of cinema, watching their favourite movies or exploring new cinematic adventures. In this game, the living room becomes a

theatre, and the rainy day becomes an opportunity to indulge in a day of cinematic delights. Movie Marathon Day offers a break from the routine and allows children to dive into a world of imagination and storytelling. Whether they choose to watch classic animated films, action-packed adventures, or heart-warming family movies, the day becomes a celebration of the art of cinema. The movie marathon can be themed around a specific genre, character, or series, adding an element of excitement and cohesion to the day's entertainment. Children can dress up as their favourite movie characters or

create movie-themed crafts to enhance the movie-watching experience. As children indulge in their movie selections, they engage with stories from different cultures and time periods, fostering empathy and a deeper understanding of diverse perspectives. Movies provide a window into worlds beyond their own, sparking curiosity and broadening their horizons. Parents and caregivers can join in the movie marathon, sharing the joy of cinematic storytelling with their children. By watching movies together, adults create moments of shared enjoyment and bonding, strengthening the family connection. Moreover, Movie Marathon Day offers a valuable opportunity for discussions and reflections. After each movie, children can share their thoughts and feelings, discussing the characters, themes, and lessons learned. These discussions promote critical thinking and encourage children to express their opinions and ideas.

C. Baking and Cooking Fun

Get ready to don aprons and unleash culinary creativity with "Baking and Cooking Fun," a game that celebrates the joy of kitchen adventures on a rainy day. In this game, children become little chefs, exploring the magic of ingredients and the art of cooking and baking. Baking and cooking activities offer a host of benefits beyond just satisfying hunger. As children measure, mix, and follow recipes, they engage with math concepts such as measurement, fractions, and temperature. Baking, in particular, introduces the science of chemical reactions as ingredients transform into delectable treats. From simple cookie recipes to elaborate cake decorating projects, the kitchen becomes a playground of culinary exploration. Children can experiment with different flavours, textures, and ingredients, turning the rainy day into a gastronomic adventure.

Baking and cooking also encourage teamwork and collaboration. Children can involve family members or friends, dividing tasks and working together to create delicious masterpieces. The shared experience creates moments of joy

and pride in their culinary achievements. Moreover, the fruits of their labor become a delightful reward, as children savor the taste of their home-made treats. Baking and cooking activities promote a sense of accomplishment and encourage children to take pride in their abilities. Parents and caregivers play an essential role in Baking and Cooking Fun, offering guidance and support in the kitchen. By sharing family recipes or trying new dishes together, adults create cherished moments of bonding and culinary exploration. Furthermore, Baking and Cooking Fun can extend beyond the rainy day, as children develop newfound skills and interest in the culinary arts. As they grow older, they can take on more challenging recipes and even experiment with creating their own unique dishes.

D. Science Fiction Day

Prepare for a journey to the far reaches of the imagination with "Science Fiction Day," where children explore the wonders of science fiction through books, movies, and imaginative play. In this game, the rainy day becomes a portal to futuristic worlds and fantastical adventures. Science Fiction Day offers a rich array of science fiction books and movies to capture children's imaginations. From intergalactic space odysseys to time-travelling adventures, science fiction introduces children to concepts of technology, outer space, and the future. Encouraging children to read science fiction books nurtures a love for reading and a passion for learning about science and technology. Books by classic science fiction authors like Isaac Asimov and Jules Verne or contemporary authors like Neil Gaiman and Madeleine L'Engle offer a diverse range of stories to explore.

Science fiction movies, whether animated or live-action, create captivating visual experiences. They transport children to alien worlds, futuristic cities, and parallel dimensions, sparking their imagination and curiosity about the universe. Science Fiction Day is also an opportunity for children to engage in imaginative play as they become astronauts, aliens, or time travellers. Using simple props like cardboard spaceships or futuristic gadgets, they bring science fiction stories to life in their own creative way. Parents and caregivers can actively participate in Science Fiction Day, sharing their favourite science fiction books and movies or engaging in imaginative play with their children. By fostering curiosity and celebrating the wonders of science fiction, adults encourage children to dream big and embrace the possibilities of the future.

E. Dance Party Extravaganza

Step into the realm of "Dance Party Extravaganza," where children let loose and dance their hearts out to their favourite tunes. In this game, the living room transforms into a dance floor, and the rainy day becomes a celebration of movement, rhythm, and joy. Dance Party Extravaganza offers a break from the rainy day doldrums, infusing the atmosphere with energy and excitement. Children can curate their dance playlists or explore different music genres, discovering new beats and rhythms to move to.

The dance floor becomes a space for self-expression, as children let go of inhibitions and allow the music to guide their movements. Dancing encourages physical activity and boosts mood, releasing endorphins that elevate their spirits. This dance extravaganza can be a solo performance or a group affair, with family members or friends joining in the fun. Dancing together fosters a sense of connection and shared joy, as children celebrate the power of music and movement. Additionally, Dance Party Extravaganza is an opportunity for children to explore different dance styles and cultures. They can try out hip-hop moves, dance to Latin rhythms, or experiment with classical ballet poses, broadening their appreciation for the art of dance. Parents and caregivers can be dance partners or enthusiastic spectators, cheering on the dance moves and celebrating the children's dance prowess. By creating a positive and encouraging environment, adults instil confidence and a sense of accomplishment. Moreover, Dance Party Extravaganza is an excellent form of physical activity, especially on a rainy day when outdoor play is not possible. It provides an outlet for children's energy and a means to stay active even within the confines of their home.

In conclusion, Rainy Day Activities offer a delightful array of indoor adventures that brighten up even the dreariest of days. From the enchanting Indoor Camping Adventure to the cinematic delights of

Movie Marathon Day, from the creative joys of Baking and Cooking Fun to the imaginative worlds of Science Fiction Day, and from the energetic Dance Party Extravaganza to the cozy pleasures of reading books and telling stories, each activity celebrates the joy of unstructured play and creativity. As children engage in these activities, they experience the wonders of play and learn valuable life skills, from creativity and collaboration to critical thinking and self-expression. Rainy Day Activities remind children that even on rainy days, there are opportunities for joy, exploration, and connection within the comfort of their home. So, let the

magic of Rainy Day Activities infuse indoor play with excitement, imagination, and moments of togetherness. As children embark on these indoor adventures, they discover that rainy days are not to be dreaded but cherished for the delightful opportunities they offer for play, learning, and celebration.

Chapter 7

Managing Screen Time

In the digital age, managing screen time has become an essential aspect of parenting and care giving. As children are exposed to an ever-increasing array of digital devices and online content, finding a healthy balance between screen time and other activities is crucial for their well-being and development. In this chapter, we explore the art of managing screen time, offering valuable insights and practical strategies to ensure that children's time with screens is both enjoyable and balanced.

A. Balancing Indoor Play and Technology

The key to managing screen time effectively lies in striking a balance between indoor play and technology. While screens offer a myriad of entertainment and educational opportunities, it's essential to ensure that children also engage in diverse indoor activities that promote physical, social, and imaginative development. Indoor play can encompass a wide range of activities, from creative art projects and imaginative play to board games, puzzles, and physical games. Encouraging children to explore various indoor activities not only helps to reduce excessive screen time but also fosters their creativity, problem-solving skills, and social interaction. Parents and caregivers play a pivotal role in modelling this balance. By actively engaging in indoor play and setting aside time for screen-free activities with their children, adults demonstrate the importance of diversifying leisure time and embracing a variety of play experiences.

Moreover, creating dedicated play spaces or play corners within the home can inspire children to gravitate towards engaging in indoor activities. These designated spaces can be stocked with age-appropriate toys, books, and craft supplies, creating an inviting environment for exploration and play. As children shift between screen time and indoor play, it's crucial to encourage open communication about their experiences and interests. By asking about their favourite activities and showing interest in their digital and non-digital pursuits, adults build a stronger connection and gain insight into their children's preferences.

B. Screen-Free Days and Benefits

Introducing screen-free days into the weekly routine is a valuable strategy for managing screen time and encouraging alternative activities. On these days, digital devices are set aside, and children are encouraged to explore a world beyond screens.

Screen-free days offer numerous benefits. They provide a break from constant screen exposure, giving children's eyes and brains a chance to rest and recharge. Additionally, screen-free days foster creativity and imagination, as children seek new ways to entertain themselves without relying on digital devices.

During screen-free days, children may rediscover the joy of outdoor play, engage in physical activities, read books, or pursue hobbies that they might have put aside during excessive screen time. These moments of exploration and discovery enrich their lives and provide valuable opportunities for learning and growth. Parents and caregivers can participate in screen-free days, making them a family-wide commitment. By turning off digital devices and engaging in screen-free activities together, adults create a supportive environment that reinforces the importance of balancing screen time with other experiences. Moreover, screen-free days offer an opportunity for meaningful family bonding. Whether it's cooking together, embarking on nature walks, or playing board games, the shared experiences on screen-free days create lasting memories and strengthen family connections.

C. Setting Rules for Screen Time

Establishing clear and consistent rules for screen time is essential for managing digital device use effectively. By setting boundaries and expectations, children gain a sense of structure and develop responsible digital habits. When setting screen time rules, consider factors such as age-appropriate content, duration of use, and time of day. Different age groups have different needs and sensitivities, so tailor the rules to suit the developmental stage of each child. Consistency is key in enforcing screen time rules. By adhering to the established guidelines, adults create a predictable environment and help children internalize healthy screen habits. Creating a screen time schedule can be beneficial, as it offers a sense of routine and prevents screen time from encroaching on other important activities, such as meal times, outdoor play, or family time.

While setting limits on screen time is essential, it's also essential to provide context and explain the reasons behind the rules. By discussing the importance of balancing screen time with other activities, children gain a deeper understanding of the rationale behind the rules. Parents and caregivers can involve children in the process of setting screen time rules. By seeking their input and discussing their preferences, adults empower children to be active participants in managing their screen time.

D. Engaging Alternatives to Screens

Encouraging engaging alternatives to screens is a key component of managing screen time effectively. By offering a diverse range of activities, adults provide children with a wealth of options for play, learning, and exploration.

Reading: Cultivating a love for reading is one of the most valuable alternatives to screen time. Whether it's fiction, non-fiction, or graphic novels, books offer endless opportunities for imagination, learning, and emotional development.

Creative Arts: Engaging in creative arts such as drawing, painting, crafting, or playing musical instruments stimulates children's creativity and self-expression. These activities also provide a sense of accomplishment and pride in their creations.

Outdoor Play: Encouraging outdoor play is vital for physical health and emotional well-being. Whether it's riding bikes, playing sports, or exploring nature, outdoor activities offer opportunities for exercise, social interaction, and a connection with the natural world.

Board Games and Puzzles: Board games and puzzles are excellent group activities that promote problem-solving, strategy, and cooperation. They also create opportunities for family bonding and friendly competition.

Role-Playing and Imaginative Play: Encouraging imaginative play fosters creativity and empathy. Whether it's pretending to be pirates, doctors, or astronauts, role-playing allows children to explore different roles and scenarios.

Cooking and Baking: Involving children in the kitchen encourages them to develop valuable life skills and fosters an appreciation for healthy eating. Cooking and baking also provide opportunities for creativity and experimentation with different ingredients.

Physical Play and Exercise: Encouraging physical play and exercise is vital for children's overall health and well-being. Whether it's dancing, yoga, or simple games like tag, physical activities release energy and promote a positive mood.

Science Experiments and Exploration: Stimulating children's curiosity with science experiments or nature exploration cultivates a love for learning and an understanding of the world around them.

Writing and Journaling: Encouraging writing and journaling promotes self-expression and emotional processing. Children can write stories, keep journals, or engage in creative writing.

Volunteer and Community Service: Involving children in volunteer work and community service fosters empathy, compassion, and a sense of responsibility towards others.

By offering a diverse range of engaging alternatives to screens, adults empower children to explore their interests and passions, building a well-rounded foundation for their physical, intellectual, and emotional development.

In conclusion, managing screen time is an important aspect of parenting and care giving in the digital age. By balancing indoor play and technology, introducing screen-free days, setting clear rules for screen time, and offering engaging alternatives to screens, adults can create a healthy and balanced approach to digital device use. As children learn to manage their screen time and explore a diverse range of activities, they develop valuable life skills, build strong family connections, and cultivate a love for learning, play, and creativity. With mindful guidance and support, children can navigate the digital world while embracing the wonders of the real world, fostering a harmonious and fulfilling relationship with technology.

Chapter 8
Parental Involvement and Safety

Parental involvement and safety are crucial aspects of fostering a positive and enriching play environment for children. As parents and caregivers, our active participation in our children's play experiences not only strengthens the parent-child bond but also ensures that their playtime is safe, age-appropriate, and conducive to learning and social development. In this chapter, we delve into the importance of parental involvement and safety, offering valuable insights and practical strategies to create a nurturing and secure play environment for our children.

A. Bonding Through Indoor Games

Indoor games provide a wonderful opportunity for parents and caregivers to bond with their children. Engaging in play together fosters a sense of closeness and connection, creating cherished memories that last a lifetime.

Board Games and Card Games: Board games and card games are excellent options for family play. They offer moments of laughter, friendly competition, and shared excitement. Whether it's rolling dice in a classic board game or strategising during a card game, playing together strengthens the parent-child relationship.

Building and Pretend Play: Joining children in building activities, such as with blocks or LEGO, encourages creativity and imagination. Parents can actively participate in constructing elaborate structures, engaging in pretend play scenarios, and exploring the wonders of the imaginative world together.

Puzzle Solving: Solving puzzles as a team enhances problem-solving skills and promotes collaborative efforts. Parents can offer guidance and encouragement during puzzle-solving sessions, fostering a sense of achievement when completing challenging puzzles.

Art and Craft Projects: Getting involved in art and craft projects allows parents and children to express their creativity together. Whether it's painting, drawing, or crafting, the shared experience of creating art strengthens the emotional bond between parents and children.

Physical Activities: Participating in physical activities, such as dancing, yoga, or indoor obstacle courses, provides opportunities for movement, laughter, and playfulness. Parents can be enthusiastic participants in these activities, inspiring children to stay active and enjoy physical play.

B. Ensuring a Safe Play Environment

Creating a safe play environment is essential for children's well-being and security during playtime. As parents and caregivers, our role in ensuring a safe space for play involves vigilance, assessment, and proactive measures.

Childproofing: Childproofing the play area is paramount, especially for younger children. Ensuring that sharp objects, choking hazards, and potentially dangerous items are out of reach helps prevent accidents and injuries.

Supervision: Regular supervision during playtime allows parents to intervene if any safety concerns arise. Close supervision is particularly important for young children who may not fully grasp the potential risks of certain activities.

Secure Furniture: Securing furniture, such as bookshelves and dressers, to the wall prevents them from tipping over and causing harm to children. Heavy or unstable furniture can be a hazard, especially in homes with young explorers.

Safe Toys: Providing age-appropriate and safe toys is essential. Parents should carefully read labels and select toys that are suitable for their child's age and developmental stage. Checking for potential choking hazards and sharp edges is also crucial.

Electronic Devices: When children use electronic devices, parents should ensure that they are age-appropriate and equipped with parental controls. Setting time limits for screen use helps prevent excessive screen time.

Emergency Preparedness: Familiarizing children with emergency procedures, such as exit routes and safety drills, instils a sense of preparedness and reassurance.

C. Age-Appropriate Games and Activities

Choosing age-appropriate games and activities is fundamental in promoting children's development and ensuring their safety. Tailoring play experiences to their age and developmental stage allows children to engage in activities that are challenging yet attainable, boosting their confidence and competence.

Cognitive Development: For young children, games that focus on colors, shapes, and numbers foster cognitive development. Puzzles with larger pieces

and matching games are excellent choices.

Language Skills: Encouraging language development can be achieved through storytelling, word games, and imaginative play. Parents can initiate conversations and ask open-ended questions to stimulate language skills.

Gross Motor Skills: Activities that promote gross motor skills, such as hopping, skipping, or playing catch, are vital for physical development. Outdoor play and indoor obstacle courses provide opportunities for active movement.

Fine Motor Skills: Fine motor skills can be enhanced through activities like drawing, coloring, and using play-dough. These activities help refine hand-eye coordination and manual dexterity.

Social Skills: Cooperative games and activities encourage teamwork, cooperation, and empathy. Parents can organize group games or role-playing scenarios to promote positive social interactions.

Emotional Development: Games that involve storytelling or emotional expression allow children to explore their feelings and emotions in a safe and supportive environment.

D. Encouraging Cooperative Play

Cooperative play is a valuable aspect of children's social development, teaching them important skills such as communication, problem-solving, and empathy. As parents and caregivers, we can actively encourage and facilitate cooperative play among children.

Group Activities: Organizing group activities, such as team-based games or art projects, promotes cooperation and teamwork. Children learn to work together towards a common goal and celebrate their collective achievements.

Role-Playing: Role-playing scenarios that involve cooperation and collaboration allow children to practice social skills and empathize with others' perspectives. Parents can participate in role-playing to model positive interactions and problem-solving.

Building Empathy: Encouraging children to take turns and share during playtime cultivates empathy and consideration for others. Parents can provide

gentle guidance in resolving conflicts and finding compromises.

Communication Skills: Facilitating communication during play helps children express their thoughts and feelings effectively. Open-ended questions and active listening create an environment where children feel heard and understood.

Building Friendships: Arranging play-dates with peers allows children to engage in cooperative play outside the family unit. Parents can facilitate interactions and support the development of positive friendships.

Praise and Encouragement: Praising children for their cooperation and positive interactions reinforces the value of teamwork and encourages them to continue engaging in cooperative play.

By actively involving ourselves in our children's play experiences and prioritizing their safety, we create a supportive and nurturing play environment that fosters their physical, social, and emotional development. As parents and caregivers, our presence and engagement during playtime are invaluable gifts that enrich our children's lives and strengthen the parent-child bond. Through mindful involvement and safety measures, we lay the foundation for positive play experiences that contribute to our children's holistic growth and well-being.

Chapter 9

Handling Challenges and Conflicts

Playtime is not always smooth sailing, and challenges and conflicts can arise among children during their play experiences. As parents and caregivers, our role in guiding children through these challenging moments is vital for their emotional development and social growth. In this chapter, we explore effective strategies for handling challenges and conflicts during playtime, fostering positive resolutions and nurturing valuable life skills.

A. Dealing with Sibling Rivalry

Sibling rivalry is a common occurrence in many households, especially when children engage in play together. Siblings may experience jealousy, competition, and conflicts over toys, attention, and perceived favouritism. As parents and caregivers, addressing sibling rivalry with empathy and fairness is essential for creating a harmonious play environment.

Individual Attention: Spending one-on-one time with each child can help alleviate feelings of competition for attention. Engaging in activities that cater to each child's interests and strengths fosters a sense of individuality and specialness.

Encourage Teamwork: Encouraging siblings to work together on projects or cooperative games promotes a sense of camaraderie and shared accomplishments. Highlighting the benefits of collaboration can help reduce the intensity of rivalry.

Conflict Resolution: Teach siblings how to resolve conflicts peacefully and respectfully. Encourage active listening, the use of "I" statements, and finding compromises to address disagreements.

Fairness and Equality: Demonstrating fairness and treating each child equally is crucial in reducing sibling rivalry. Avoid showing favouritism and ensure that each child's needs and feelings are valued and respected.

Problem-Solving: Guide siblings in problem-solving together when conflicts arise. Rather than intervening immediately, encourage them to work through their differences independently, with adult supervision if needed.

Celebrate Individual Achievements: Celebrate each child's individual achievements and strengths to build their self-esteem and reduce the need for constant comparison.

B. Managing Competitive Play

Competitive play can be both exciting and challenging for children. While healthy competition can encourage motivation and goal-setting, it's essential to manage competitive play to avoid potential conflicts and negative emotions.

Emphasize Sportsmanship: Teach children the importance of good sportsmanship, which includes fair play, respect for opponents, and handling both wins and losses graciously.

Set Clear Rules: Establish clear rules for competitive games and activities to ensure a level playing field and prevent misunderstandings.

Encourage Friendly Competition: Emphasize the idea of competing against oneself rather than always comparing with others. Encourage children to focus on personal growth and improvement.

Address Unsportsmanlike Behaviour: Address any unsportsmanlike behaviour immediately and guide children on appropriate ways to handle frustrations and disappointments.

Emphasize Effort Over Outcome: Encourage children to focus on their effort and hard work rather than solely on the outcome or winning.

Model Positive Behaviour: Demonstrate positive and respectful behaviour during competitive play, serving as a role model for children.

C. Resolving Disagreements and Tears

Disagreements and tears are natural aspects of play, especially when children are learning to navigate social interactions and emotions. As parents and caregivers, our role is to help children work through these challenges and develop effective conflict resolution skills.

Active Listening: Listen attentively to each child's perspective during conflicts, showing empathy and understanding their feelings.

Validate Emotions: Validate the emotions of each child, acknowledging their feelings without judgment.

Teach Problem-Solving: Guide children in finding solutions to their disagreements, encouraging compromise and finding win-win solutions.

Time-Outs: Offer time-outs for cooling off during heated conflicts, allowing children to regain composure before addressing the issue.

Mediation: Act as a mediator when needed, helping children navigate conflicts with empathy and fairness.

Provide Comfort: Offer comfort and reassurance to children who are upset or in tears, letting them know that it's okay to express their emotions.

D. Teaching Sportsmanship and Fair Play

Sportsmanship and fair play are essential values for children to learn during playtime. These values not only apply to sports but also to all aspects of life, including social interactions and relationships.

Praise Sportsmanship: Praise and acknowledge instances of good sportsmanship and fair play, reinforcing these positive behaviours.

Discuss Emotions: Have open discussions about emotions and how to handle them during play, emphasizing the importance of self-control and respect for others.

Teach Respect: Teach children to respect opponents, teammates, and the rules of the game.

Handle Losses Gracefully: Teach children to handle losses with grace and dignity, focusing on the effort they put forth rather than the outcome.

Model Fair Play: Model fair play and good sportsmanship in your interactions with others, including your children.

Foster an Inclusive Environment: Encourage inclusivity and ensure that all children feel welcome and valued during play.

By proactively addressing challenges and conflicts during playtime, parents and caregivers equip children with valuable life skills, including communication, empathy, and problem-solving. These skills extend far beyond playtime and

serve as a foundation for their social and emotional development throughout life. Through mindful guidance and support, we create a positive and nurturing play environment where children can learn, grow, and develop into confident, respectful, and empathetic individuals.

Conclusion

In "Playing Games: Keeping Kids Entertained Indoors - Age Group 4 to 12 Years Old," we have embarked on a journey to discover the wonders of indoor play and its limitless potential to entertain, educate, and bond families together. Throughout this book, we have explored a diverse array of engaging games and activities that cater to children's interests, abilities, and developmental stages, ensuring that every child finds joy and fulfilment in their playtime.

From active games that get children moving and grooving to creative activities that nurture their imagination, from educational games that spark curiosity and learning to technology-free games that promote social interactions, we have strived to provide a holistic approach to indoor play. Additionally, we have delved into the magic of rainy day activities, fostering a sense of adventure and exploration even when the weather is less than ideal.

We have discussed the significance of parental involvement and safety, recognizing the pivotal role parents and caregivers play in nurturing their children's play experiences. By actively engaging in playtime, creating a safe environment, and fostering cooperative play, we strengthen the parent-child bond and promote essential life skills that extend beyond playtime.

Throughout this journey, we have embraced the challenges and conflicts that may arise during play, offering practical strategies for dealing with sibling rivalry, managing competitive play, resolving disagreements, and teaching sportsmanship. By equipping children with conflict resolution skills and guiding them with empathy and fairness, we empower them to navigate the complexities of social interactions with confidence and compassion.

As we conclude this book, I invite readers to embrace the joy and significance of indoor play in shaping children's growth, development, and happiness. I encourage parents, caregivers, and educators to actively participate in children's play experiences, fostering a nurturing and stimulating environment that enhances their physical, cognitive, and emotional well-being.

I wholeheartedly request our readers to share their feedback and review this book. Your valuable insights and opinions are essential in our ongoing quest to enhance the play experiences of children around the world. I hope that "Playing Games: Keeping Kids Entertained Indoors" has inspired families to create cherished memories and moments of togetherness, forging connections that last a lifetime.

May the magic of play continue to unfold in the lives of children, guiding them to explore, learn, and grow with boundless curiosity and creativity. Let us join hands in celebrating the wonder of play and its power to shape the future generation, one game at a time.

Thank you for embarking on this playful journey with us, and we look forward to hearing from you!

Happy playing!

Simi Subhramanian

Milton Keynes UK
Ingram Content Group UK Ltd.
UKHW020750210823
427162UK00013B/249

9 798223 048015